P9-EDI-725

SOLO-SPEARE!:

SHAKESPEAREAN MONOLOGUES FOR STUDENT ACTORS

EDITED BY
Lindsay Price

Theatrefolk
Original Playscripts

Solo-Speare!:
Shakespearean Monologues for Student Actors
Copyright © 2003 Lindsay Price

CAUTION: This play is fully protected under the copyright laws of Canada and all other countries of the Universal Copyright Convention and is subject to royalty. Changes to the script are expressly forbidden without written consent of the author. Rights to produce, film, or record, in whole or in part, in any medium or in any language, by any group *amateur or professional*, are fully reserved.

Interested persons are requested to apply for **amateur** rights to:

Theatrefolk
PO Box 1064
Crystal Beach, ON, L0S 1B0
Canada
Tel 1-866-245-9138
Fax 1-877-245-9138
e-mail: tfolk@theatrefolk.com
website: www.theatrefolk.com

Those interested in **professional** rights may contact the author c/o the above address.

No part of this script covered by the copyrights hereon may be reproduced or used in any form or by any means - graphic, electronic or mechanical - without the prior written permission of the author. Any request for photocopying, recording, or taping shall be directed in writing to the author at the address above.

Printed in the USA
ISBN 1-894870-44-1

Editor's Notes

This collection gives you all the tools you need to put together the best Shakespearean monologue. Dynamic speeches, lesser-known characters (anyone can do "Romeo, Romeo" or "To be or not to be!") and all the help you'll need with acting suggestions, background info, and vocabulary.

General Shakespeare Performance Tips: Understand what you're saying. Look up every word you don't understand. The more you know, the more you can convey. Read the play, or at the very least the scenes leading up to the monologue. Have fun with it — try different interpretations of the words and images. You only have a couple of minutes to make a impression.

Go Big and Bold!

TWO GENTLEMEN OF VERONA ACT 1 SCENE 2

Background:	The two "Gentlemen of Verona" are Valentine and Proteus. At this point in the play, Proteus is in love with Julia.
	Julia has been hiding her feelings for Proteus to the point where she tears up a letter she has just received from him. As soon as she is alone, however, she dives for the pieces of paper scattered on the floor. She does love Proteus and this is the first time she speaks her feelings aloud.
Character:	Julia is a young upper-class woman of Verona. It's interesting to see Julia acting so foolishly, when it is not in her normal nature.
Tips:	This is a fun, physical piece. Make sure you have a torn-up letter to play with. It's very funny the way she talks to these little pieces of paper as if they were Proteus.
	It's also funny that this speech is a declaration of love, and yet she's crawling around on the floor kissing "each several paper for amends." This means she's "making up" to the pieces of paper! At the end of the monologue Julia folds a piece of paper so that the two names (Proteus and Julia) appear to "kiss." There's a lot of room for humour here.
	Julia is usually a refined, dignified woman - what happens to such a woman when she becomes lovesick? How does she change?
	Notice how she treats herself in the speech. She calls her hands "injurious wasps" for tearing the letter and she chastises herself by throwing down any piece of paper with her name on it.
	It's always interesting when people say things for the first time. Make sure Julia's feelings sound new and fresh — not rehearsed.
	How will you end the piece? With a loving sigh? A kiss of the paper? With a laugh? Maybe you kiss the paper and it doesn't taste so great.

VOCABULARY

writ	written	**thrice**	three times
bosom	chest	**thence**	there
heal'd	healed	**lo**	look
sovereign	kingly. Meaning "supreme" in this context.	**sith**	since

JULIA

O hateful hands, to tear such loving words!
Injurious wasps, to feed on such sweet honey
And kill the bees that yield it with your stings!
I'll kiss each several paper for amends.
Look, here is **writ** 'kind Julia.' Unkind Julia!
As in revenge of thy ingratitude,
I throw thy name against the bruising stones,
Trampling contemptuously on thy disdain.
And here is writ 'love-wounded Proteus.'
Poor wounded name! My **bosom** as a bed
Shall lodge thee till thy wound be thoroughly **heal'd**;
And thus I search it with a **sovereign** kiss.
But twice or **thrice** was 'Proteus' written down.
Be calm, good wind, blow not a word away
Till I have found each letter in the letter,
Except mine own name: that some whirlwind bear
Unto a ragged fearful-hanging rock
And throw it **thence** into the raging sea!
Lo, here in one line is his name twice writ,
'Poor forlorn Proteus, passionate Proteus,
To the sweet Julia:' that I'll tear away.
And yet I will not, **sith** so prettily
He couples it to his complaining names.
Thus will I fold them one on another:
Now kiss, embrace, contend, do what you will.

HENRY VI PART I ACT 5 SCENE 4

Background:	Henry the Sixth is a three-part story of civil war (part of the "War of the Roses" cycle) and the war between England and France. In this monologue, Joan of Arc is speaking to the Earl of Warick and the Duke of York, who have just condemned her to death for being a witch.
Character:	"La Pucelle" means "The Maid."
	Joan of Arc is an historical figure from the 1400's. As a young girl she heard voices telling her she was going to help drive the English out of France. Astonishingly, she was able to convince the powers-that-be of this and went on to lead several battles. She was eventually captured and sold to the English. They feared her and burned her at the stake. She was only nineteen.
	This monologue combines two different speeches from **Act V scene four**.
	Joan is portrayed in French history as a brave soldier and a saint. The English thought she was a witch. Shakespeare did not see Joan as a brave soldier or a heroine. He has Joan beg for her life earlier in the scene by pretending she's pregnant as pregnant women could stay their execution until they gave birth. She also denies she is a country girl because of her relationship with God.
Tips:	Read all of **Act V scene four** to see the different tactics Joan uses to try and stop her execution.
	There is a lot of information available about Joan of Arc; do some research and form your own opinion about how she should be portrayed. Despite Shakespeare's opinion of the character, you can certainly choose to play her any way you like!
	Here are some ways to play the speech: as a crazed witch who thinks herself above her condemners, as a heroine bravely going to her death, as a young girl who is terrified of dying. Which is the most dramatic? Which will have the most impact on your audience?
	Think about the setting of the speech. How does the monologue change if Joan can see the stake being prepared for her? Does she panic or grow in strength?
	Lastly, don't forget she is speaking to two men. Experiment with addressing different parts of the speech to each of her listeners.

VOCABULARY

begotten	born	**straight**	immediately
swain	rustic, country person	**reflex**	reflect
progeny	descendants	**make abode**	live
celestial	heavenly	**environ**	form a ring around

JOAN LA PUCELLE (JOAN OF ARC)

First, let me tell you whom you have condemn'd:
Not me **begotten** of a shepherd **swain**,
But issued from the **progeny** of kings;
Virtuous and holy; chosen from above,
By inspiration of **celestial** grace,
To work exceeding miracles on earth.
I never had to do with wicked spirits:
But you, that are polluted with your lusts,
Stain'd with the guiltless blood of innocents,
Corrupt and tainted with a thousand vices,
Because you want the grace that others have,
You judge it **straight** a thing impossible
To compass wonders but by help of devils.

Then lead me hence; with whom I leave my curse:
May never glorious sun **reflex** his beams
Upon the country where you **make abode**;
But darkness and the gloomy shade of death
Environ you, till mischief and despair
Drive you to break your necks or hang yourselves!

ROMEO AND JULIET ACT 2 SCENE 5

Background:	Romeo and Juliet are from rival families: the Montagues and the Capulets. The two meet, fall madly in love, and decide to marry — all in an evening.
	It is the next day. Juliet waits impatiently (it has been three hours) for her nurse to return from meeting with Romeo. He is to give the nurse a time and place for he and Juliet to be married.
Character:	Juliet is fourteen years old in the story. She has lead a sheltered life and is currently "engaged" to Paris even as she plans a secret marriage to Romeo. She is impulsive and full-of-life.
	Keep in mind that the story takes place even before Shakespeare's time: marriage at such a young age was not uncommon or unheard of.
Tips:	If you are unfamiliar with the story, read **Act I scene five** to see where Romeo and Juliet meet, and then read **Act II scene two** for the famous balcony scene. You'll need to be familiar with these scenes to understand the full extent of Juliet's emotions in the monologue.
	The story of *Romeo and Juliet* is universal — the ultimate story of defying parental wishes and taking young love to the extreme. Do you know anyone who has acted like Juliet? (Perhaps not to this extent, though!) Can you think of a way to bring that person's attitude and energy to the speech?
	This monologue is filled with extremes. Juliet zooms from frustration, to depression, to happiness, and back again. Use these emotions to find the comic potential in the speech. How would you physicalize each of these emotions? One suggestion is to use a chair as a prop. Juliet could repeatedly try to sit and be ladylike, only to be so agitated she keeps getting up.
	Remember that this is one of Juliet's happiest moments: she is to be married to the man she loves and she has no idea of what's to come. Don't foreshadow the end.
	There are a lot of interesting images in this monologue from the frowning hills, to the nurse being thrown like a ball. How can you best show these images to you audience? Think of specific actions and the way you use your voice.

VOCABULARY

perchance	maybe	**bandy**	throw
louring	frowning, scowl, sullen	**feign**	pretend
nimble-pinion'd	agile bird's wing	**unwieldy**	slow, clumsy
Cupid	Roman God of Love		

JULIET

The clock struck nine when I did send the nurse;
In half an hour she promised to return.
Perchance she cannot meet him: that's not so.
O, she is lame! Love's heralds should be thoughts,
Which ten times faster glide than the sun's beams,
Driving back shadows over **louring** hills:
Therefore do **nimble-pinion'd** doves draw love,
And therefore hath the wind-swift **Cupid** wings.
Now is the sun upon the highmost hill
Of this day's journey, and from nine till twelve
Is three long hours, yet she is not come.
Had she affections and warm youthful blood,
She would be as swift in motion as a ball;
My words would **bandy** her to my sweet love,
And his to me:
But old folks, many **feign** as they were dead;
Unwieldy, slow, heavy and pale as lead.
O God, she comes!

ANTONY AND CLEOPATRA ACT I SCENE 2

Background:	Charmian, Iras, Alexas and others of Cleopatra's court gather to hear a soothsayer tell their fortunes.
Character:	Charmian is one of Cleopatra's closest maids — so close that Charmian often speaks her mind to the Queen. This monologue gives a good indication of her personality; she is young and doesn't think too much about the future.

This monologue is a combination piece — it combines some of Charmian's lines (and a speech of Iras') in her interaction with the soothsayer to make a complete piece.

It's always interesting to look at the comic characters in tragedies. Shakespeare knew that the story can't be all doom and gloom. |
| **Tips:** | A very light-hearted piece. Have fun with it and with Charmian's personality.

Read the full scene (**Act II scene five**) to see what else the Soothsayer foretells for Charmian. She's not happy about what the Soothsayer has to say!

At the beginning of the monologue we hear Charmian's side of her conversation with the Soothsayer. Make sure you pause for a moment when Charmian asks a question so she may hear the answer. Use these moments to show Charmian's personality through physical action. She's clearly impatient to hear a good fortune. How can you show this?

Charmian hopes that Alexis has an infertile wife who dies and then many more wives who cheat on him; this is what would make Alexis a cuckold. What are Charmian's feelings for Alexis? Does she dislike him or is she teasing him? What do you imagine Alexis is doing during her speech?

When Charmian calls on Isis what is she doing physically? Does she go on her knees? Does she throw her arms to the sky? She's clearly having fun but it would add a sense of variety to the piece if you add some ritualistic movement to her lines. Do some research to find out how ancient Egyptians prayed. |

VOCABULARY

Alexas	one of Cleopatra's attendants	**Octavius Caesar**	one of the rulers of Rome
th'Queen	the Queen - Cleopatra, also Charmian's mistress.	**Isis**	Egyptian Goddess
is't	is it	**cuckold**	husband of an adulteress
forenoon	morning	**beseech**	plead
Herod of Jewry	a Jewish King	**knave**	dishonest man

CHARMIAN

Lord **Alexas**, sweet Alexas, most anything Alexas, almost most absolute Alexas, where's the soothsayer that you prais'd so to **th'Queen**? Is this the man, **is't** you, sir, that know things? Good sir, give me good fortune. *(she sticks out her hand to have it read)* I shall yet be fairer than I am? Wrinkles forbid! I shall be more beloving than beloved? I had rather heat my liver with drinking. Good, now, some excellent fortune! Let me be married to three things in a **forenoon**, and widow them all. Let me have a child at fifty, to whom **Herod of Jewry** may do homage. Find me to marry me with **Octavius Caesar** and companion me with my mistress. I shall out live the lady whom I serve? Oh, excellent, I love long life better than figs. Alexas, come, his fortune, his fortune! O, let him marry a woman that cannot go, sweet **Isis**, I beseech thee! And let her die too, and give him a worse! and let worst follow worse, till the worst of all follow him laughing to his grave, fifty-fold a **cuckold**! Good Isis, hear me this prayer, though thou deny me a matter of more weight; good Isis, I **beseech** thee! Dear goddess, hear that prayer of the people! For, as it is a heartbreaking to see a handsome man loose-wived, so it is a deadly sorrow to behold a foul **knave** uncuckolded: therefore, dear Isis, keep decorum, and fortune him accordingly! Amen.

TROILUS AND CRESSIDA ACT 3 SCENE 2

Background:	In the midst of the Trojan war, (fought between the Trojans and the Greeks) Troilus loves Cressida. Up to now, Cressida has rebuked him. Finally, Cressida shares her feelings with him.
Character:	Cressida is a young Trojan woman. She comes across as witty and intelligent. She has spurned Troilus' advances because she believes that "men prize the thing ungain'd more than it is." **(Act I scene two)** Even when she declares her love she thinks it's a mistake. It's interesting that she describes the months she's been in love with Troilus as "weary." What does this tell you about her character?
Tips:	This speech is hard for Cressida to say. This should be evident in the way you perform it. Even in this moment of love she mocks herself for being in love. When she says "we fools" she refers to women who share their feelings of love. Cressida is also on a rollercoaster of emotion. She has kept her feelings pent up inside; this is the first time these words have come out. See how she describes her thoughts as "unbridled children, grown too headstrong for their mother." How will you show this image physically? Think of Cressida's emotional state as you deliver the speech, particularly the line "I have loved you night and day for many weary months." How will you say this line? Quickly, to get it out? Slowly? With a laugh? With her eyes shut tight so she can't see Troilus' reaction? With the weariness she talks about? Look at the journey Troilus and Cressida take up to this point. We hear about Troilus' love for Cressida right off the top **(Act I scene one)** where he talks about being "mad in Cressid's love." In **Act I scene two** Cressida is still playing hard-to-get when she tells Pandarus (her uncle) that Troilus "is not Hector." Finally, Troilus gets Pandarus to orchestrate a meeting **(Act III scene one)** where Cressida first describes lovers as "monsters" but then gives in to her feelings.

VOCABULARY

in faith	in truth	**rapture**	highest delight
unbridled	uncontrollable	**repent**	regret
blabb'd	blabbed, spoken out	**soul of counsel**	my deepest thoughts
woo'd	enticed, courted, flattered	**stop my mouth**	kiss me

CRESSIDA

Boldness comes to me now, and brings me heart.
Prince Troilus, I have loved you night and day
For many weary months.
Hard to seem won: but I was won, my lord,
With the first glance that ever — pardon me —
If I confess much, you will play the tyrant.
I love you now; but not, till now, so much
But I might master it: **in faith**, I lie;
My thoughts were like **unbridled** children, grown
Too headstrong for their mother. See, we fools!
Why have I **blabb'd**? Who shall be true to us,
When we are so unsecret to ourselves?
But, though I loved you well, I **woo'd** you not;
And yet, good faith, I wish'd myself a man,
Or that we women had men's privilege
Of speaking first. Sweet, bid me hold my tongue,
For in this **rapture** I shall surely speak
The thing I shall **repent**. See, see, your silence,
Cunning in dumbness, from my weakness draws
My very **soul of counsel! Stop my mouth**.

AS YOU LIKE IT ACT 3 SCENE 5

Background:	As You Like It explores love and shows many different types of relationships. Phebe and Silvius are one of the couples. They are often described as examples of "Pastoral love" because of their rustic backgrounds and the exaggerated nature of Silvius' passion.
	The relationship between the two is rocky at best. Silvius has professed his love to Phebe and her response is not positive. In the moment before this speech, Silvius asks Phebe to not be his executioner when she bitterly tells him she does not love him.
Character:	Phebe is a shepherdess with a cold heart. She clearly sees herself as "above" Silvius, a fellow shepherd. Why is that?
	This speech is the first we see of Phebe — what kind of impression does she make? In **Act III scene four** Corin describes Phebe as having "the red glow of scorn and proud disdain."
Tips:	In order to bring some variety to the speech, find other emotions for Phebe besides her obvious anger and scorn. For example, some girls flirt with boys who they know are in love with them, just so they can scorn them again. Does Phebe seem like that sort of girl? Where could you fit this type of action into the speech?
	Read about Silvius' great love for Phebe in **Act II scene three.**
	When Phebe talks about her eyes as murderers is she being serious or sarcastic? She goes to the extreme in this monologue to point out to Silvius what a ridiculous notion this is. Keep this in mind for lines like "'Tis pretty, sure and very probable."
	The extent of Phebe's cruelty is evident in the moment after this monologue. Phebe convinces Silvius to deliver a love letter to another man for her. That's pretty cruel!

VOCABULARY

thy	your	**counterfeit to swoon**	pretend to faint
thee	you	**cicatrice**	a scar
mine	my	**impressure**	impressions
shut their coward gates on atomies		close their lids to protect themselves from the tiniest particles	

PHEBE

I would not be **thy** executioner:
I fly thee, for I would not injure **thee**.
Thou tell'st me there is murder in **mine** eye:
'Tis pretty, sure, and very probable,
That eyes, that are the frail'st and softest things,
Who **shut their coward gates on atomies**,
Should be call'd tyrants, butchers, murderers!
Now I do frown on thee with all my heart;
And if mine eyes can wound, now let them kill thee:
Now **counterfeit to swoon**; why now fall down;
Or if thou canst not, O, for shame, for shame,
Lie not, to say mine eyes are murderers!
Now show the wound mine eye hath made in thee:
Scratch thee but with a pin, and there remains
Some scar of it; lean but upon a rush,
The **cicatrice** and capable **impressure**
Thy palm some moment keeps; but now mine eyes,
Which I have darted at thee, hurt thee not,
Nor, I am sure, there is no force in eyes
That can do hurt.

OTHELLO ACT 4 SCENE 3

Background:	Othello's mind is poisoned against Desdemona (his wife) and believes she is an adulteress. She, on the other hand, has done nothing wrong and cannot understand the changes in her husband. Emilia watches the disintegration of Othello and Desdemona's relationship. She sees Othello insult Desdemona, hit her, and call her a whore. Emilia hits the mark when she says Othello is acting like a jealous husband. In the moment before this monologue Emilia helps Desdemona get ready for bed. She sees Desdemona as a despondent shell, unable to understand Othello's change. Desdemona believes no woman could be unfaithful to her husband. This monologue is Emilia's response; she believes, under the right circumstances, women could and should be unfaithful.
Character:	Emilia is married to Iago (the man who poisons Othello's mind) and is Desdemona's closest maid. She suffers from a conflict of loyalties: Emilia steals Desdemona's handkerchief at Iago's request and denies knowing its whereabouts to Desdemona. Yet Emilia wholeheartedly defends Desdemona when Othello wants to know **(Act IV scene two)** if Desdemona has been behaving deceptively. Emilia's character is a complete contrast to Desdemona. She is of lower class, is more cynical, and more realistic — particularly when it comes to men. Emilia says **(Act III scene four)** that men "are all but stomachs and we all but food."
Tips:	The most important question to ask is whether Emilia is an innocent bystander who is fooled by Iago or whether she is a willing participant. Your decision will flavour how you perform the piece. Read all of **Act IV scene three** to familiarize yourself with the tension leading up to the monologue. What emotional state is Emilia in during this monologue? Is she calm? Agitated? What does she think is going to happen to Desdemona? It's clear in the piece Emilia is sometimes referring to Othello. Is there anywhere where she can refer to Iago? What is their marriage like? When she talks of "foreign laps" is she suggesting that Iago has been unfaithful? This is something Othello clearly hasn't done.

VOCABULARY

foreign laps	other women	**palates**	tastes
peevish	spiteful	**doth**	does
scant	skimp	**is't**	is it
galls	exasperations	**errs**	makes mistakes

EMILIA

But I do think it is their husbands' faults
If wives do fall: say that they slack their duties,
And pour our treasures into **foreign laps**,
Or else break out in **peevish** jealousies,
Throwing restraint upon us; or say they strike us,
Or **scant** our former having in despite;
Why, we have **galls**, and though we have some grace,
Yet have we some revenge. Let husbands know
Their wives have sense like them: they see and smell
And have their **palates** both for sweet and sour,
As husbands have. What is it that they do
When they change us for others? Is it sport?
I think it is: and **doth** affection breed it?
I think it doth: **is't** frailty that thus **errs**?
It is so too: and have not we affections,
Desires for sport, and frailty, as men have?
Then let them use us well: else let them know,
The ills we do, their ills instruct us so.

TWELFTH NIGHT ACT 2 SCENE 2

Background:	After a shipwreck, Viola lands alone in Illyria and must pretend she's a boy until she can get her bearings. She becomes "Cesario" and hires herself out to Count Orseno as a page. Orseno sends "Cesario" to express his love to a lady named Olivia. Though Olivia wants nothing to do with Orseno, she does find herself falling for "Cesario."
	In the moment before this speech, Olivia's steward Malvolio returns a ring to Viola. Olivia has told Malvolio it's from Orseno and she doesn't want it. But the ring is really a love token from Olivia. Viola realizes Olivia has fallen in love with "Cesario" and doesn't know what to do.
Character:	Viola is the heroine of *Twelfth Night*. She is smart, brave, and quick-thinking. Having said that, she is certainly out of her element in this monologue and with her disguise.
	She is also in love with Orseno.
Tips:	Viola directly refers to her previous interaction with Olivia in this monologue. Read **Act I scene five** to familiarize yourself with the conversation. You will see how Viola starts to get into her disguise.
	Viola is amazed and a bit freaked-out that someone fell for her disguise ("fortune forbid my outside have not charmed her!") Play this amazement during the speech. What are the different ways Viola can say "she loves me, sure?" She can say it with shock, with a laugh, or with horror, to name a few. Try out some different ways.
	Viola also knows the absurdity and humour of her situation. Her disguise, which at first is a comfort, is now somewhat of a trap. Find places for her to laugh at herself and the position she finds herself in.
	Physically Viola is playing a man, but she is also alone. Does she ever forget herself during the speech and start to move as a woman? Does she catch herself?
	Before she found herself in Illyria, Viola was an upper-class woman. Can this background inform the speech, especially since she's now playing a servant?

VOCABULARY

made good view of me	looked at me closely	**proper-false**	a handsome man who is false inside
methought	I thought	**fadge**	work out
churlish messenger	she means Malvolio	**dote**	love
the pregnant enemy	the devil	**thriftless**	useless

VIOLA

I left no ring with her: what means this lady?
Fortune forbid my outside have not charm'd her!
She **made good view of me**; indeed, so much,
That sure **methought** her eyes had lost her tongue,
For she did speak in starts distractedly.
She loves me, sure; the cunning of her passion
Invites me in this **churlish messenger**.
None of my lord's ring! Why, he sent her none.
I am the man: if it be so, as 'tis,
Poor lady, she were better love a dream.
Disguise, I see, thou art a wickedness,
Wherein **the pregnant enemy** does much.
How easy is it for the **proper-false**
In women's waxen hearts to set their forms!
Alas, our frailty is the cause, not we!
For such as we are made of, such we be.
How will this **fadge**? My master loves her dearly;
And I, poor monster, fond as much on him;
And she, mistaken, seems to **dote** on me.
What will become of this? As I am man,
My state is desperate for my master's love;
As I am woman, — now alas the day! —
What **thriftless** sighs shall poor Olivia breathe!
O time! Thou must untangle this, not I;
It is too hard a knot for me to untie!

KING JOHN ACT 3 SCENE 1

Background:	France and England are locked in war. Blanch is set up as a peace offering: she will marry Lewis, son of King Phillip of France. But when peace is broken, Blanch is caught between the two sides.
Character:	Blanch is the King of Spain's daughter and King John's niece.
	Duty plays a big part of Blanch's character and her lot in the story. She is willing to marry Lewis because it is called for.
	Duty is also her downfall; she fears death is in her future because she cannot decide between her duty to her family and her duty to Lewis.
Tips:	This monologue combines two of Blanch's speeches in the scene. In both sections, Blanch speaks directly to Lewis, who has just called for his father (King Phillip of France) to bear arms and resume fighting. Lewis trades his love for Blanch with the stronger love of his country.
	The wedding between Lewis and Blanch is set up in a previous scene **(Act II scene one)** where Lewis makes clear he loves Blanch. Is there a moment in the monologue where Blanch can see Lewis turn his back on her as he turns his back on the peace between England and France? How would she react to that?
	There are a lot of conflicting emotions in this monologue. Blanch is torn between her duty as a wife and her duty towards her family. She has been given up for a specific cause, but the cause is moot when the war between the two countries resumes. How does this make Blanch feel? Defeated? Bitter? Resigned? What emotions will you play?
	Note the tug-of-war imagery in the line "They swirl asunder and dismember me." How will you show this?
	At the end of the speech she talks to some of the other characters that surround her:
	Her <u>Uncle</u> is King John.
	Her <u>Father</u> is King Phillip (now by marriage.)
	Her <u>Granddam</u> (grandmother) is Queen Elinor, King John's mother, who is against the wedding and peace.

VOCABULARY

churlish	unpleasant	**o'ercast**	overcast
clamours	loud sustained noise	**adieu**	goodbye
pomp	the music for the wedding	**withal**	with
ne'er	never	**asunder**	apart

BLANCH

To arms?
Upon thy wedding-day?
Against the blood that thou hast married?
What, shall our feast be kept with slaughter'd men?
Shall braying trumpets and loud **churlish** drums,
Clamours of hell, be measures to our **pomp**?
O husband, hear me! Ay, alack, how new
Is husband in my mouth! Even for that name,
Which till this time my tongue did **ne'er** pronounce,
Upon my knee I beg, go not to arms
Against mine uncle.

The sun's **o'ercast** with blood: fair day, **adieu**!
Which is the side that I must go **withal**?
I am with both: each army hath a hand;
And in their rage, I having hold of both,
They swirl **asunder** and dismember me.
Husband, I cannot pray that thou mayst win;
Uncle, I needs must pray that thou mayst lose;
Father, I may not wish the fortune thine;
Grandam, I will not wish thy fortunes thrive:
Whoever wins, on that side shall I lose
Assured loss before the match be play'd.
Lewis, with you, with you my fortune lies.
There where my fortune lives, there my life dies.

ROMEO AND JULIET ACT 4 SCENE 3

Background:	Romeo Montague and Juliet Capulet are from rival families. The two have met, fallen in love, and married.
	Romeo and Juliet's romance turns sour. Tybalt (Juliet's cousin) challenges Romeo, Romeo kills Tybalt, and is thus banished from Verona.
	Meanwhile, Juliet's father decides that Juliet will marry Paris as quickly as possible. Juliet tells her father of her secret marriage to Romeo, which doesn't go over well.
	Juliet goes to the Friar, who comes up with a plan: Juliet will take a potion which will make her seem dead. She will be put into the family tomb and, by the time she wakes up, the Friar will rescue her with Romeo by his side.
	As Juliet prepares to take the potion her imagination runs away with her as she agonizes over what could go wrong.
Character:	Juliet is often described as a silly girl. Even though the love between Romeo and Juliet seems exaggerated, hasty and immature, it takes a lot of courage (or perhaps insanity?) to take a drug and know you're going to wake up in a tomb surrounded by dead people.
Tips:	Emotionally, Juliet should switch between the terror of what's going to happen to her and her undying love for Romeo.
	Everyone's imagination goes wild at times. In the monologue, Juliet imagines that the Friar is trying to kill her for marrying Romeo, and that her cousin Tybalt is going to rise from the dead.
	Picture yourself in a situation where you have imagined the worst possible scenario. How did it affect your breathing? Your actions? Did you speak slowly or quickly?
	Allow Juliet to see the horrors around her — particularly a newly-dead Tybalt. What does he look like?
	Make sure you have a vial or small jar on which to focus your horror.

VOCABULARY

methinks	I think	**ere**	before
hath still	has always	**conceit**	notion, idea
redeem	recover	**green in earth**	freshly buried
stifled	smothered	**mandrakes**	A plant that was once believed to have magical powers. It supposedly gave a shriek when pulled.
healthsome	wholesome		

JULIET

What if it be a poison, which the friar
Subtly hath minister'd to have me dead,
Lest in this marriage he should be dishonour'd,
Because he married me before to Romeo?
I fear it is: and yet, **methinks**, it should not,
For he **hath still** been tried a holy man.
How if, when I am laid into the tomb,
I wake before the time that Romeo
Come to **redeem** me? There's a fearful point!
Shall I not then be **stifled** in the vault,
To whose foul mouth no **healthsome** air breathes in,
And there die strangled **ere** my Romeo comes?
Or, if I live, is it not very like,
The horrible **conceit** of death and night,
Together with the terror of the place,
As in a vault, an ancient receptacle,
Where for these many hundred years the bones
Of all my buried ancestors are packed:
Where bloody Tybalt, yet but **green in earth**,
Lies festering in his shroud; where, as they say,
At some hours in the night spirits resort.
Alack, alack, is it not like that I,
So early waking, what with loathsome smells,
And shrieks like **mandrakes'** torn out of the earth,
That living mortals, hearing them, run mad:
O, look! Methinks I see my cousin's ghost
Seeking out Romeo, that did spit his body
Upon a rapier's point: stay, Tybalt, stay!
Romeo, Romeo, Romeo. Here's drink. I drink to thee.

OTHELLO ACT 4 SCENE 3

Background:	Othello's mind is poisoned against his wife, Desdemona, and believes she is an adulteress. She, on the other hand, has done nothing wrong and cannot understand the changes in her husband. In the moment before this monologue, Othello has ordered Desdemona to bed. She gets ready as requested with her maid Emilia. Desdemona is at the end of her rope and doesn't know what to do.
Character:	Desdemona is a strange character. At the beginning of the play she is independent and outspoken — she defies her father and defends her marriage to Othello. See this different side of Desdemona in **Act I scene three.** Once she arrives in Cyprus she seems to become more of a stereotype: submissive, pure, and faithful. Is it her blind devotion to Othello, no matter what he does, that seems to trap her in the end?
Tips:	This monologue is very different from the other monologues. It has a slower, more morose tone, and there's a great deal of subtext with the impending doom of Othello's approach. It is the quiet before the storm; the sorrow of a lost marriage; a very disturbing moment. The song will play an important part in the tone of the piece. What melody will you use? Come up with something in a minor key, it should be quite wistful and match her mood. What is she thinking about as she sings? In the next scene Othello will smother Desdemona to death with a pillow. Do she have an idea of what's to come? This monologue takes place in Desdemona's chamber as she gets ready for bed. Read the complete scene **(Act IV scene three)** to grasp the desperation of the moment. Note in the scene how Desdemona asks Emilia to dress her in her wedding dress, and to put the linen from her wedding night on the bed. She also tells Emilia that she wants this linen to be used as her shroud.

VOCABULARY

forsake	give up, desert, abandon	couch	sleep
'twas	It was	bode	foretell, predict
prithee	please	wouldst thou	would you
dispatch	leave quickly	troth	truth, on my word
moe	more	beshrew me	"the Devil take me"

DESDEMONA

(Singing) The poor soul sat sighing by a sycamore tree,
Sing all a green willow:
Her hand on her bosom, her head on her knee,
Sing willow, willow, willow.

(Speaking) My mother had a maid call'd Barbara:
She was in love, and he she loved proved mad
And did **forsake** her: she had a song of 'willow;'
An old thing **'twas**, but it express'd her fortune,
And she died singing it: that song to-night
Will not go from my mind; I have much to do,
But to go hang my head all at one side,
And sing it like poor Barbara. *(to Emilia)* **Prithee, dispatch.**

(Singing) Sing all a green willow must be my garland.
Let nobody blame him; his scorn I approve,
(Speaking) Nay, that's not next. Hark! who is't that knocks?
(Singing) I call'd my love false love; but what said he then?
Sing willow, willow, willow:
If I court **moe** women, you'll **couch** with moe men!

(Speaking) So, get thee gone; good night. Mine eyes do itch;
Doth that **bode** weeping?
I have heard it said so. O, these men, these men!
Dost thou in conscience think, tell me, Emilia,
That there be women do abuse their husbands
In such gross kind?
Wouldst thou do such a deed for all the world?
In **troth**, I think thou wouldst not.
Beshrew me, if I would do such a wrong
Good night, good night: heaven me such uses send,
Not to pick bad from bad, but by bad mend!

TWELFTH NIGHT ACT 2 SCENE 3

Background:	Maria is part of a gang of sorts with Sir Toby (Olivia's uncle) and Sir Andrew (friend of Sir Toby, who is trying to woo Olivia).
	The scene takes place at Olivia's house where Sir Toby and Sir Andrew are carousing late into the night. Maria comes out to tell them to be quiet.
	In the moment before, Olivia's steward Malvolio has yelled at the crew, especially Maria. It is this humiliation that motivates her to make a fool out of Malvolio.
	They are going to trick Malvolio into thinking Olivia is in love with him. Maria will write a letter and fake Olivia's handwriting. In the letter it will seem that Olivia loves a man who is very much like Malvolio.
Character:	Maria is Olivia's lady-in-waiting.
	Maria is more like one of the guys than one of the girls. She's a fun character: mischievous, a tease, and the brains of the group. She is a sharp contrast to Olivia, who could be characterized as a "proper woman."
	Compare Maria, who is a girl who runs with the boys, to Viola, who must hide her femininity and become a boy.
Tips:	Maria is in complete control. She has the plan and she knows it's going to succeed. This is no fragile girl.
	Look at **Act II scene five** for the actual letter Maria writes.
	Remember that it is very late at night. This should affect the way that Maria speaks. Give the monologue a quiet, conspiratorial air.
	When she talks about the "fool make a third," she is referring to Feste the Clown, another lowbrow character.
	There is a lot of unfamiliar vocabulary in the speech. Make sure you understand exactly what she's saying!

VOCABULARY

youth of the count's	Viola (aka Cesario)	**cons state without book**	he memorizes books
thy lady	Olivia	**swarths**	masses
gull	dupe	**epistles**	letters
nayword	proverb	**wherein**	in which
common recreation	laughingstock	**feelingly personated**	exactly described
puritan	someone very moral	**phsyic**	medicine
time-pleaser	a flatterer	**construction**	interpretation

MARIA

Sweet Sir Toby, be patient for tonight: since the **youth of the count's** was today with **thy lady**, she is much out of quiet. For Monsieur Malvolio, let me alone with him: if I do not **gull** him into a **nayword**, and make him a **common recreation**, do not think I have wit enough to lie straight in my bed: I know I can do it.

Marry, sir, sometimes he is a kind of **puritan**. The devil a puritan that he is, or any thing constantly, but a **time-pleaser**; an affectioned ass, that **cons state without book** and utters it by great **swarths**: the best persuaded of himself, so crammed, as he thinks, with excellencies, that it is his grounds of faith that all that look on him love him; and on that vice in him will my revenge find notable cause to work.

I will drop in his way some obscure **epistles** of love; **wherein**, by the colour of his beard, the shape of his leg, the manner of his gait, the expressure of his eye, forehead, and complexion, he shall find himself most **feelingly personated**. I can write very like my lady your niece: on a forgotten matter we can hardly make distinction of our hands.

Sport royal, I warrant you: I know my **physic** will work with him. I will plant you two, and let the fool make a third, where he shall find the letter: observe his **construction** of it. For this night, to bed, and dream on the event. Farewell.

TROILUS AND CRESSIDA ACT 5 SCENE 3

Background:	The story takes place in the middle of the Trojan war — a battle between the Trojans and the Greeks. Hector, a Trojan Hero, is about to go onto the battlefield. Cassandra knows that if he fights, he will die. If he dies, the Trojans will lose the war. In the moment before, Hector's wife tries to stop him from fighting. Hector is too brash and stubborn to listen. When Cassandra enters, Hector has thrown a vow to the gods: "bid my trumpets." He will fight. Cassandra speaks in response to Hector's haste and stubbornness.
Character:	Cassandra is a character from Greek mythology. She was given the gift of prediction from Apollo, but when she spurned his advances, he "twisted" the gift. Cassandra can still see the future, but no one believes her. She is often portrayed as a "mad" and unstable character.
Tips:	There are very high stakes here. Not only is Hector's life at stake, but all of Troy's. The most important motivation in the monologue is convincing Hector not to leave. Cassandra tends to come off as a bit of a shrieker. When she appears in the play she always seems to be wailing! Resist that urge. Find places to wail, and then explore places to express the opposite emotion. It's more effective if Cassandra earnestly tries to convince Hector to stay. For example, the line "Behold: distraction, frenzy and amazement" presents such an interesting image. You don't want to lose it in a piercing shriek. This is a difficult monologue physically because Cassandra is surrounded by people. As you rehearse, make sure you know where each person is so it's clear to the audience. She mentions some of the characters by name. They are: Priam: The Trojan king (Cassandra and Hector's father) Andromache: Hector's wife Hecuba: Priam's wife (Cassandra and Hector's mother) When does Hector leave in the speech? How would his leaving influence the way you deliver the end of the monologue?

VOCABULARY

peevish	irritable	**vents**	openings
abhorr'd	detested	**dolours**	sorrow
eye turns pale	as in death		

CASSANDRA

The gods are deaf to hot and **peevish** vows:
They are polluted offerings, more **abhorr'd**
Than spotted livers in the sacrifice.
It is the purpose that makes strong the vow;
But vows to every purpose must not hold:
Unarm, sweet Hector.
Lay hold upon him, Priam, hold him fast:
He is thy crutch; now if thou lose thy stay,
Thou on him leaning, and all Troy on thee,
Fall all together.
O, farewell, dear Hector!
Look, how thou diest! Look, how thy **eye turns pale**!
Look, how thy wounds do bleed at many **vents**!
Hark, how Troy roars! How Hecuba cries out!
How poor Andromache shrills her **dolours** forth!
Behold: distraction, frenzy and amazement,
Like witless antics, one another meet,
And all cry, Hector! Hector's dead! O Hector!
Farewell: yet, soft! Hector! Take my leave:
Thou dost thyself and all our Troy deceive.

TWO GENTLEMEN OF VERONA ACT 4 SCENE 4

Background:	The two "Gentlemen of Verona" are Valentine and Proteus, both on their way to Milan.
	At the beginning of the play Proteus swears his love for Julia, who gives him a ring to remember her by. But he falls in love with Sylvia as soon as he gets to Milan.
	Meanwhile, Julia decides she can't wait to hear from Proteus and decides to follow him. A woman can't travel alone so she disguises herself as a boy named "Sebastian." Ironically, she gets to Milan, is hired by Proteus as a page, and learns Proteus no longer loves her.
	In the moment before this monologue Proteus gives Julia's ring to "Sebastian" to deliver to Sylvia as a love token. Julia must act as a messenger to convey Proteus' love to Sylvia with her own ring.
Character:	Julia is a young woman of Verona. She is dignified and very loyal. In this monologue she is dressed as Sebastian, a page.
Tips:	Julia is forlorn and despondent in this speech; don't play that all the way through. Find some variety to play so the monologue isn't all one note. Find places for her to demonstrate her love for Proteus, even though he's been so awful to her.
	To find this love, read scenes for both Proteus and Julia from earlier in the play. Proteus describes his feelings for Julia in **Act I scene one**; Julia describes her feelings in **Act I scene two**. You should also read her monologue on **page 4** of this collection. The two characters have a good-bye moment in **Act II scene two**. This is the scene in which Julia gives Proteus the ring.
	Use a real ring as a prop. What can Julia do with the ring? Some choices are: polish it, wear it, kiss it, spit on it, take out her frustrations on it, etc.

VOCABULARY

do such	deliver such	**obtain**	get
thou hast	you have	**master**	Proteus is Sebastian's master
thy	your	**woo**	to court, to romance
despiseth	despises, hates	**speed**	succeed

JULIA

How many women would **do such** a message?
Alas, poor Proteus! **Thou hast** entertain'd
A fox to be the shepherd of **thy** lambs.
Alas, poor fool! Why do I pity him
That with his very heart **despiseth** me?
Because he loves her, he despiseth me;
Because I love him, I must pity him.
This ring I gave him when he parted from me,
To bind him to remember my good will;
And now am I, unhappy messenger,
To plead for that which I would not **obtain**,
To carry that which I would have refused,
To praise his faith which I would have dispraised.
I am my **master**'s true-confirmed love;
But cannot be true servant to my master,
Unless I prove false traitor to myself.
Yet will I **woo** for him, but yet so coldly
As, heaven it knows, I would not have him **speed**.

A MIDSUMMER NIGHT'S DREAM ACT 3 SCENE 2

Background:	Lysander loves Hermia. Hermia loves Lysander. Demetrius loves Hermia. Helena loves Demetrius.
	This is the lovers' subplot of A *Midsummer Night's Dream*. All four end up in the forest. Mischief from a fairy (Puck) causes both boys to fall in love with Helena. Helena thinks the boys are making fun of her since she knows they both love Hermia and not her.
Character:	Helena is the epitome of unrequited love.
	Now, all of a sudden, the object of her desire professes his love for her. This monologue is her reaction. What does this tell you about Helena? Does she truly believe Demetrius would ever love her?
	Read her monologue at the end of **Act I scene one**, as well as her conversation with Demetrius in **Act II scene one** to get a grasp of Helena's character.
Tips:	Helena has had an unhappy journey throughout the play and this speech is the climax of her frustration. How can you physicalize her frustration? Being a "lady" is all about containment and I can really see Helena almost exploding in this monologue.
	The speech is almost like a child's temper tantrum — that might be fun to play with! Having said that, don't just rant and rave with the piece. Find the humour, find the unexpected.
	Helena is also a girl who lacks confidence. Her best friend Hermia is the popular girl who always gets the guy. What would that do to a person physically?
	To use a modern illustration, Helena comes across as a third-wheel — the friend who never has a date. This is most evident in her scene with Lysander and Hermia in **Act I scene one**.
	Another thing you could do is research productions of A *Midsummer Night's Dream* and discover how different actresses portray Helena.
	Lastly, remember that Lysander and Demetrius are both drugged and are looking at her with complete adoration. How does that affect the way Helena delivers the speech?

VOCABULARY

show	appearance	**trim**	fine
superpraise	over praise	**derision**	ridicule, mockery
parts	qualities	**extort**	torture

HELENA

O spite! O hell! I see you all are bent
To set against me for your merriment:
If you were civil and knew courtesy,
You would not do me thus much injury.
Can you not hate me, as I know you do,
But you must join in souls to mock me too?
If you were men, as men you are in **show**,
You would not use a gentle lady so;
To vow, and swear, and **superpraise** my **parts**,
When I am sure you hate me with your hearts.
You both are rivals, and love Hermia;
And now both rivals, to mock Helena:
A **trim** exploit, a manly enterprise,
To conjure tears up in a poor maid's eyes
With your **derision**! None of noble sort
Would so offend a virgin, and **extort**
A poor soul's patience, all to make you sport.

AS YOU LIKE IT ACT 3 SCENE 5

Background:	Rosalind is hiding in the woods with her cousin Celia because she has been banished from court. As a safety precaution, she is disguised as a boy.

In this monologue Rosalind chastises Phebe (see **page 15**) for the way she treats Silvius, the shepherd. She also tries to get Silvius to find another girl because he is so much better than Phebe. |
| **Character:** | Rosalind is a girl pretending to be a boy (Ganymede). Since she is a boy, she gets to speak and behave in ways she wouldn't get away with as a girl.

Rosalind is also in love with Orlando, but because of her disguise cannot share her feelings with him, even though she knows that he loves her.

She is the central character of the play. She's strong, witty, and bright but also very lovesick! She knows love can be foolish and yet loves being in love. It makes for an interesting contrast. She is not perfect. |
| **Tips:** | The first thing to remember is that Rosalind is pretending to be a boy in front of other characters; this needs to be reflected in the way you move and speak. Does she ever slip up and do something as a girl when she shouldn't?

Rosalind's first line is in answer to a line Phebe gives to Silvius: "As till that time I shall not pity thee."

Read the whole scene **(Act III scene five)** to fully understand Rosalind's point of view.

Also look at **Act II scene three** where Rosalind sees Silvius for the first time and remarks "Jove, Jove, this shepherd's passion, is much upon my fashion." She relates her feelings for Orlando to his feelings for Phebe. It'll give you some good background to understand why Rosalind is so angry with Phebe in this monologue.

An easy trap to fall into with this monologue is to play it for anger from beginning to end. Rosalind is a wit; she teases rather than yells. |

VOCABULARY

than without a candle may go dark to bed	Phebe doesn't have enough beauty to light the dark	**wherefore**	why
sale-work	something done carelessly	**foggy south**	south wind
'Od's	God save	**glass**	mirror
entame	subdue	**lineaments**	features of the face

ROSALIND

And why, I pray you? Who might be your mother,
That you insult, exult, and all at once,
Over the wretched? What though you have no beauty, —
As, by my faith, I see no more in you
Than without candle may go dark to bed —
Must you be therefore proud and pitiless?
Why, what means this? Why do you look on me?
I see no more in you than in the ordinary
Of nature's **sale-work**. **'Od's** my little life,
I think she means to tangle my eyes too!
No, faith, proud mistress, hope not after it:
'Tis not your inky brows, your black silk hair,
Your bugle eyeballs, nor your cheek of cream,
That can **entame** my spirits to your worship.
(to Silvius) You foolish shepherd, **wherefore** do you follow her,
Like **foggy south** puffing with wind and rain?
You are a thousand times a properer man
Than she a woman: 'tis such fools as you
That makes the world full of ill-favour'd children:
'Tis not her **glass**, but you, that flatters her;
And out of you she sees herself more proper
Than any of her **lineaments** can show her.
(to Phebe) But, mistress, know yourself: down on your knees,
And thank heaven, fasting, for a good man's love:
For I must tell you friendly in your ear,
Sell when you can: you are not for all markets:
Cry the man mercy; love him; take his offer:
Foul is most foul, being foul to be a scoffer.
So take her to thee, shepherd: fare you well.

TROILUS AND CRESSIDA ACT 4 SCENE 2

Background:	The play takes place during the Trojan war. As part of a trade, Cressida is to be "sold" to the Greek side. Her uncle Pandarus has just told Cressida the news. Unfortunately this moment happens right after Cressida and Troilus have expressed their feelings for one another.
	This trade was orchestrated by Cressida's father (Calchas), a Trojan who defected to the Greek side. It is her father's wish to bring Cressida to him.
Character:	Think about Cressida's relationship with her father. It can't be ordinary, especially since her father is a traitor. When she talks about "forgetting" her father, she is denying everything between them: blood, kin, love, and soul.
	There is a tug-of-war inside of her between her duty to go and her desire to stay with Troilus. She knows deep inside that, despite her grandiose statements, she has to go. She has no free will.
Tips:	This monologue contains new information for Cressida. Not only must she leave her home to go to the enemy side, she must also leave the man she has just expressed her love for. Read her monologue on **page 12**.
	Her life has changed forever. This calls for large emotion: shock, fear, anger, love, and disgust. Don't pick one, play them all.
	It would be easy to yell the whole monologue but it would not be as effective as portraying a wide range of emotions. Is there some place for Cressida to have a quiet moment? Perhaps she starts out small and gains intensity.
	In this monologue Cressida is so distraught she talks about wrecking the traditional images of beauty: tearing out her hair and scratching her cheeks. This should give you an indication about what Cressida normally looks like.
	Keep this in mind as well — Cressida played hard to get for so long; if she had shared her feelings sooner, she could have had more time with Troilus. Is she upset with herself in this moment?

VOCABULARY

consanguinity	having the same blood, of the same family		
Cressid's	Cressida - the word is shortened for the rhythm of the line		
kin	family	**sounding**	crying

CRESSIDA

O you immortal gods! I will not go.
I will not, uncle: I have forgot my father;
I know no touch of **consanguinity**;
No **kin** no love, no blood, no soul so near me
As the sweet Troilus. O you gods divine!
Make **Cressid's** name the very crown of falsehood,
If ever she leave Troilus! Time, force, and death,
Do to this body what extremes you can;
But the strong base and building of my love
Is as the very centre of the earth,
Drawing all things to it. I'll go in and weep,
Tear my bright hair and scratch my praised cheeks,
Crack my clear voice with sobs and break my heart
With **sounding** Troilus. I will not go from Troy.

CYMBELINE ACT 3 SCENE 4

Background	Imogen disobeys her father by secretly marrying Posthumus, who is banished from Britain.
	While in Italy, Posthumus wagers that Imogen cannot be seduced by the nobleman, Jachimo. Imogen is no fool and refuses Jachimo's advances. Jachimo, however, tricks Posthumus into thinking the seduction was successful. Furious, Posthumus writes a letter to Pisanio, his servant, and instructs him to kill Imogen.
	This monologue takes place in the country, where Pisanio has taken Imogen, supposedly to see Posthumus. But Pisanio has brought Imogen there to kill her. Pisanio loses his nerve and hands over Posthumus' letter to Imogen instead. She is understandably shocked and overcome.
Character	Imogen is a princess, daughter to Cymbeline, King of Britain. She is intelligent, brave, and loyal. Despite the play's title, Imogen is the play's central figure.
	One of Imogen's chief strengths is her ability to keep her head up despite the constant bullying from the other characters. She is hated by her step-mother, lusted after by her step-brother, her husband is banished by her father, and her husband orders her killed under false pretences.
Tips	Start the monologue at "False to his bed!" for a shorter piece.
	You need two props: the letter and a dagger. What can Imogen do with the letter after she had read it? Crumple it? Tear it? Throw it at Pisanio?
	Imogen is stunned to find out what Posthumus thinks about her. In the moment before, she is happy and excited, thinking that she is going to see her husband.
	Allow her sense of betrayal to take several forms in the monologue — it looks fast and furious on the page but it doesn't have to be that way all the way through. When someone is in shock they are often slow and deliberate as if their brain can't compute what's happening. When she asks Pisanio to kill her, the speech should pick up speed.
	Even though Imogen refers to Jachimo and Posthumus in the monologue, neither are there. When she says "Come fellow" she is referring to Pisanio.

VOCABULARY

strumpet	prostitute	**to's**	to his
whereof	of what	**incontinency**	lacking self-restraint
surmises	suspicions	**jay**	strumpet, prostitute
twixt clock and clock	on the hour	**where't**	where it

IMOGEN

(Reads) 'Thy mistress, Pisanio, hath played the **strumpet** in my bed; the testimonies **whereof** lie bleeding in me. I speak not out of weak **surmises**, but from proof as strong as my grief and as certain as I expect my revenge. That part thou, Pisanio, must act for me, if thy faith be not tainted with the breach of hers. Let thine own hands take away her life: I shall give thee opportunity at Milford-Haven.'

False to his bed! What is it to be false?
To lie in watch there and to think on him?
To weep **'twixt clock and clock**? If sleep charge nature,
To break it with a fearful dream of him,
And cry myself awake? That's false **to's** bed, is it?
I false! Thy conscience witness: Jachimo,
Thou didst accuse him of **incontinency**;
Thou then look'dst like a villain; now methinks
Thy favour's good enough. Some **jay** of Italy
Whose mother was her painting, hath betray'd him:
Poor I am stale, a garment out of fashion;
And, for I am richer than to hang by the walls,
I must be ripp'd:--to pieces with me! O!
Men's vows are women's traitors! All good seeming,
By thy revolt, O husband, shall be thought
Put on for villany; not born **where't** grows,
But worn a bait for ladies.
Come, fellow, be thou honest:
Do thou thy master's bidding: when thou see'st him,
A little witness my obedience: look!
I draw the sword myself: take it, and hit
The innocent mansion of my love, my heart;
Fear not; 'tis empty of all things but grief;
Thy master is not there, who was indeed
The riches of it: do his bidding; strike!

TWO GENTLEMEN OF VERONA ACT 2 SCENE 6

Background:	The two "Gentlemen of Verona" are Proteus and Valentine. They both leave Verona for Milan.
	Before leaving, Proteus swears his love to Julia. But when he arrives in Milan, he falls in love with Sylvia. He knows his "best friend" Valentine is also in love with Sylvia.
	Proteus decides to pursue his new love (Sylvia) and to forget his first love (Julia). He is going to betray his best friend and tell Sylvia's father how Valentine and Sylvia were planning to sneak away.
Character:	It's hard to like Proteus. But that is what makes this speech so interesting and fun to play. Most of us cannot imagine ourselves behaving and speaking in such a manner as Proteus behaves and speaks!
	He's rash and puts love (which isn't returned) in front of everything. He even turns Love into a person in the monologue, calling on Love to help him in his quest.
	He starts the play off as a gentleman and turns into a jerk rather quickly. He's impulsive and always in the moment. He is unconcerned about how Julia will feel when she learns he no longer loves her.
	Is Proteus a villain? If so, what kind of villain is he? He's certainly not in the same league as Richard the Third but he does put his own needs above all others.
	In Greek mythology, Proteus was a sea-god who was able to change his shape. In more modern terms, the name "Proteus" means "inconstant."
Tips:	There is a conflict here between loyalty and passion.
	Read what Proteus says to Julia in **Act II scene two** and then see how quickly he forgets those words by **Act II scene four**.
	How will you perform the moment where Proteus verbalizes his betrayal of both Valentine and Julia? Is he manic? Gleeful? Filled with remorse?
	It's interesting to note how Proteus describes Julia and Sylvia. He calls Julia a "twinkling star" and Sylvia a "celestial sun." What physical actions could go with these very specific images?

VOCABULARY

foresworn	false	**pretended**	intended
provokes	urges	**cross**	thwart, stop
perjury	break an oath or promise	**drift**	upcoming event

PROTEUS

To leave my Julia, shall I be **forsworn**;
To love fair Silvia, shall I be forsworn;
To wrong my friend, I shall be much forsworn;
And even that power which gave me first my oath
Provokes me to this threefold **perjury**;
Love bade me swear and Love bids me forswear.
O sweet-suggesting Love, if thou hast sinned,
Teach me, thy tempted subject, to excuse it!
At first I did adore a twinkling star,
But now I worship a celestial sun.
I will forget that Julia is alive,
Remembering that my love to her is dead;
And Valentine I'll hold an enemy,
Aiming at Silvia as a sweeter friend.
I cannot now prove constant to myself,
Without some treachery used to Valentine.
This night he meaneth with a corded ladder
To climb celestial Silvia's chamber-window,
Myself in counsel, his competitor.
Now presently I'll give her father notice
Of their disguising and **pretended** flight;
Who, all enraged, will banish Valentine;
For Thurio, he intends, shall wed his daughter;
But, Valentine being gone, I'll quickly **cross**
By some sly trick blunt Thurio's dull proceeding.
Love, lend me wings to make my purpose swift,
As thou hast lent me wit to plot this **drift**!

ROMEO AND JULIET ACT 3 SCENE 3

Background:	Romeo falls in love with Juliet, the daughter of his family's sworn enemy. They get married after knowing each other one night. But a fight between Romeo and Tybalt (Juliet's cousin) finds Tybalt dead and Romeo banished from Verona.
	In the moment before this monologue Friar Lawrence happily relays the news of Romeo's banishment. He's happy because the punishment could have been death. Romeo feels that banishment is worse than death because he will never see Juliet again.
Character:	Romeo is sixteen years old. He is an intense fellow. Everything he does is to the extreme, including this reaction. Romeo doesn't see any other way out than the most dramatic reaction. He lacks moderation.
	Having said that, he's not afraid to stand up for himself and his family. He kills Tybalt because Tybalt killed Mercutio, Romeo's best friend.
Tips:	How can you use Romeo's intense dramatic personality to its best potential? You don't want to be over-the-top for the whole monologue — that would be hard to watch and tiring to play.
	The monologue has highs and lows, so you should contrast moments of intense drama with quiet.
	Romeo also makes some very corny and melodramatic statements. He says that heaven is here where Juliet lives and every cat, dog, and mouse gets to live in heaven, but not him. That's a bit much. Is there some comic potential? Will you play the whole thing straight or ham it up a bit?
	How do you the monologue to affect your audience? Since the piece is out of context with the rest of the play, you have some choice on how you present it.
	Remember that Romeo too has an audience: he seems to be performing his grief rather than actually living it.

VOCABULARY

hath	has	**hadst thou**	have you
carrion-flies	flies that buzz around the dead	**mean**	means
vestal	chaste	**ne'er**	never

ROMEO

Ha, banishment! Be merciful, say 'death;'
For exile **hath** more terror in his look,
Much more than death: do not say 'banishment.'
Heaven is here,
Where Juliet lives; and every cat and dog
And little mouse, every unworthy thing,
Live here in heaven and may look on her;
But Romeo may not: more validity,
More honourable state, more courtship lives
In **carrion-flies** than Romeo: they may seize
On the white wonder of dear Juliet's hand
And steal immortal blessing from her lips,
Who even in pure and **vestal** modesty,
Still blush, as thinking their own kisses sin;
But Romeo may not; he is banished:
Flies may do this, but I from this must fly:
They are free men, but I am banished.
And say'st thou yet that exile is not death?
Hadst thou no poison mix'd, no sharp-ground knife,
No sudden **mean** of death, though **ne'er** so mean,
But 'banished' to kill me? 'Banished?'
O friar, the damned use that word in hell;
Howlings attend it: how hast thou the heart,
Being a divine, a ghostly confessor,
A sin-absolver, and my friend profess'd,
To mangle me with that word 'banished'?

LOVE'S LABOURS LOST ACT 3 SCENE I

Background:	King Ferdinand invites three young men to his court with some very specific conditions: they must only sleep three hours a night, they must fast once a week, and they must swear off women.
	Of course, the last condition is very hard to follow. In this monologue Berowne talks about his sudden love for Rosaline, one of the ladies attending on the Princess of France.
	In the moment before, Berowne has just given a love letter to a servant to deliver to Rosaline.
Character:	Berowne is a young lord. He has the most trouble with the conditions imposed by King Ferdinand.
	Note: His name is "Biron" in some editions of the play.
Tips:	Read **Act II scene one** where Berowne and Rosaline first meet. You should also read the details of the pact between the four men and the conditions they must follow in **Act I scene one**.
	One of the things that amazes Berowne in this monologue is that he has fallen in love with a "common" woman, someone of a lower class than he. Rosaline does not conform to the stereotypical notions of beauty. Note his unflattering description of her "pitch-ball" eyes.
	This is one monologue where you should go over the top. Berowne is overcome with love. Note all the different silly names he comes up with for Cupid ("Dan" is another word for "Sir.")
	Berowne is normally a courteous gentlemen, but this is a moment where he is unrestrained and not himself. How does love overtake him? Is he giddy? Is very physical; running around and acting goofy? Is he melodious and romantic? Is he horrified at what is happening to him? Surprised? Amazed? It should be the first time this has ever happened to him.
	Note that Berowne's romantic declaration doesn't rhyme. This is unusual for Shakespeare.
	Remember too that as Berowne declares his love out loud he's supposed to have nothing to do with women. Is he aware that someone might discover him at any moment? Are there times in the monologue where he speaks quietly?

VOCABULARY

forsooth	in truth	**plackets**	slit in a dress, blouse, or skirt
beadle	officer	**'paritors**	officers of the court
pedant	teacher	**wightly**	pale
whimpled	blindfolded	**Argus**	a giant monster with 100 eyes
soverign	king	**Joan**	name for a common woman (like 'plain Jane')

BEROWNE

O, and I, **forsooth**, in love! I, that have been love's whip;
A very **beadle** to a humorous sigh;
A critic, nay, a night-watch constable;
A domineering **pedant** o'er the boy;
Than whom no mortal so magnificent!
This **whimpled**, whining, purblind, wayward boy;
This senior-junior, giant-dwarf, Dan Cupid;
Regent of love-rhymes, lord of folded arms,
The anointed **sovereign** of sighs and groans,
Liege of all loiterers and malcontents,
Dread prince of **plackets**, king of codpieces,
Sole imperator and great general
Of trotting **'paritors** (O my little heart)
And I to be a corporal of his field,
And wear his colours like a tumbler's hoop!
What, I! I love! I sue! I seek a wife!
A woman, that is like a German clock,
Still a-repairing, ever out of frame,
And never going aright, being a watch,
But being watch'd that it may still go right!
Nay, to be perjured, which is worst of all;
And, among three, to love the worst of all;
A **wightly** wanton with a velvet brow,
With two pitch-balls stuck in her face for eyes;
Ay, and by heaven, one that will do the deed
Though **Argus** were her eunuch and her guard:
And I to sigh for her! To watch for her!
To pray for her! Go to; it is a plague
That Cupid will impose for my neglect
Of his almighty dreadful little might.
Well, I will love, write, sigh, pray, sue and groan:
Some men must love my lady and some **Joan**.

HENRY VI PART 3 ACT 5 SCENE 6

Background:	One of the history plays in the "War of the Roses" cycle. The War of the Roses details the power struggle between two rival families as they fight for control of England.
	Henry the Sixth (a Lancaster) does not have much power; he's a weak king. So much so that he promises the throne to the opposite side (the Yorks) after his death. Therefore his sons (Richard included) are denied access to the throne.
	This monologue takes place at the end of the play. At the beginning of the scene Henry calls Richard a devil. Richard is furious about Henry's decision about the throne and has only one purpose in the scene: to kill Henry.
	In the moment before this monologue, Richard stabs Henry. Henry sinks to the ground.
Character:	Richard is described as being ugly and a cripple with a hump on his back.
	He describes his deformity in **Act III scene two**. Specifically he talks about the "mountain on (his) back" and his legs being "of an unequal size." He is determined to be king, no matter who gets in his way. No matter what the cost. For example, Richard mentions he going to find a way to kill his brothers Clarence and Edward in order to hasten his ascent to the throne.
	Richard is about to become the villain in "Richard the Third."
Tips:	The most important thing to do is keep Richard's physical state in mind as you move through the piece.
	Richard talks further about his deformities in this monologue. He says he was a breech baby ("with my legs forward") and that his appearance made the midwife wonder and the women cry because he wasn't normal-looking. Do you think Richard revels in his looks or does he wish he looked like everyone else?
	What is Richard's emotional state when he kills the king? Is he gleeful? Wrathful? In **Act III scene two** Richard talks about putting on a face for others, so we should see the true Richard in this moment. When he talks about how his sword weeps (it's dripping blood) is this a happy or sad moment for him?

VOCABULARY

mounted	as in raise to heaven	**usurp'd**	seized wrongly
purple	blood	**greybeards**	old people
house	the house of Lancaster	**pitchy**	black
thither	there	**be best**	be king

RICHARD

What! Will the aspiring blood of Lancaster
Sink in the ground? I thought it would have **mounted**.
See how my sword weeps for the poor king's death!
O! May such **purple** tears be always shed
From those that wish the downfall of our **house**.
Is any spark of life be yet remaining,
Down, down to hell; and say I sent thee **thither**,
(Richard stabs Henry again)
I, that have neither pity, love, nor fear.
Indeed, it is true that Henry told me of;
For I have often heard my mother say
I came into the world with my legs forward.
Had I not reason, think ye, to make haste,
And seek their ruin that **usurp'd** our right?
The midwife wonder'd, and the women cried
'O! Jesus bless us, he is born with teeth'
And so I was; which plainly signified
That I should snarl and bite and play the dog.
Then, since the heavens have shaped my body so,
Let hell make crook'd my mind to answer it.
I have no brother, I am like no brother;
And this word 'love,' which **greybeards** call divine,
Be resident in men like one another
And not in me: I am myself alone.
Clarence, beware; thou keep'st me from the light;
But I will sort a **pitchy** day for thee;
For I will buzz abroad such prophecies
That Edward shall be fearful of his life;
And then, to purge his fear, I'll be thy death.
King Henry and the prince his son are gone:
Clarence, thy turn is next, and then the rest,
Counting myself but bad till I **be best**.

TROILUS AND CRESSIDA ACT 5 SCENE 10

Background:	This play takes place during the Trojan war, which was fought between the Trojans and the Greeks. The Trojan hero Hector has been killed by the Greek Achilles, who then tied Hector's body to his horse and dragged it around the battlefield. Troilus has returned to Troy to relay the news.
Character:	Troilus is a solider and Hector's brother. Priam and Hecuba are Hector's parents.
Tips:	Troilus appears elsewhere in the play as a lover; here he is the consummate soldier. He is genuinely heartbroken but, as a solider, works to keep his emotions more or less under control. Does he succeed in this throughout the monologue? There are many rich images in the piece. The screech-owl Troilus mentions is not only a bird, but also the symbol of Athens (similar to eagles in the USA and beavers in Canada.) He also mentions that Hector's death will "turn Priam to stone, make wells and Niobes of the maids and wives." In mythology, Niobe cried so hard over the death of her children she turned to stone. Troilus also yells at the gods when he calls out "Frown on, you heavens." Another thing to keep in mind is that in a previous scene **(Act V scene three)** Cassandra has not only foretold Hector's death but also that his death marks Troy's loss in the war. Troilus is surrounded by Trojans during this speech. Why does he call the crowd "vile abominable tents?" He tells the crowd to go and then yells at them for leaving. Remember, Troilus is overcome with grief and not completely in his right mind. How will you show this physically? People usually internalize grief, but in this situation that wouldn't be very dramatic. Read Hector's death scene at **Act V scene eight**.

VOCABULARY

pight	pitched, as a tent	**sunder**	separate
Phrygian	Troy	**wicked**	sinful, vicious
Titan	the sun	**frenzy**	delirious fury
great-sized coward	Achilles	**woe**	bitter grief

TROILUS

Hector is slain.
He's dead; and at the murderer's horse's tail,
In beastly sort, dragg'd through the shameful field.
Frown on, you heavens, effect your rage with speed!
Sit, gods, upon your thrones, and smile at Troy!
I say, at once let your brief plagues be mercy,
And linger not our sure destructions on!
I do not speak of flight, of fear, of death,
But dare all imminence that gods and men
Address their dangers in. Hector is gone:
Who shall tell Priam so, or Hecuba?
Let him that will a screech-owl aye be call'd,
Go in to Troy, and say there, Hector's dead:
There is a word will Priam turn to stone;
Make wells and Niobes of the maids and wives,
Cold statues of the youth, and, in a word,
Scare Troy out of itself. But, march away:
Hector is dead; there is no more to say.
Stay yet. You vile abominable tents,
Thus proudly **pight** upon our **Phrygian** plains,
Let **Titan** rise as early as he dare,
I'll through and through you! And, thou **great-sized coward,**
No space of earth shall **sunder** our two hates:
I'll haunt thee like a **wicked** conscience still,
That mouldeth goblins swift as **frenzy's** thoughts.
Strike a free march to Troy! With comfort go:
Hope of revenge shall hide our inward **woe.**

TWO GENTLEMEN OF VERONA ACT 2 SCENE 3

Background:	The two "Gentlemen of Verona" are Proteus and Valentine.
	Launce is Proteus' servant. Proteus is going to Milan, and so is Launce. The monologue is about how everyone in Launce's family is sad to see Launce go, except for Crab - his dog.
Character:	Launce is a servant. He speaks in prose instead of in verse. In most productions he is always seen with his "sourest-natured" dog; a very humorous relationship.
Tips:	Even though there is quite a bit of humour in the piece, Launce takes himself and everything he does in the monologue seriously. There shouldn't be any winks to the audience about how stupid he's being. In fact, the straighter you are with the piece, the funnier it will be. A guy pretending his shoe is his mother and a stick is his sister is funny enough all on its own!
	At one point he talks about how his father (the shoe) weeps and his mother breathes. How will you show that one shoe cries and the other breathes? Be creative!
	On that note - make sure you have shoes that come off easily. Launce also needs a staff (or stick) and a hat to play all the members of his family. The humour in this piece truly comes from the physical interaction with the props.
	Launce talks about how his family is sad to see him go. How does Launce feel about going? Is he sad or excited to go on this adventure?
	You'll need a sound (like a sigh) or an action to complete the monologue. The last line doesn't quite complete the moment; you want to be sure your audience knows it's the end! Perhaps Launce can do something with the dog— either howl at it or give a growl.

VOCABULARY

proportion	part	**staff**	stick
perplexity	confusion	**wood**	distraught
cur	worthless dog	**'tis**	It is
on't	on it		

LAUNCE

I have received my **proportion**, like the prodigious son, and am going with Sir Proteus to the Imperial's court. I think Crab, my dog, be the sourest-natured dog that lives: my mother weeping, my father wailing, my sister crying, our maid howling, our cat wringing her hands, and all our house in a great **perplexity**, yet did not this cruel-hearted **cur** shed one tear: he is a stone, a very pebble stone, and has no more pity in him than a dog. Nay, I'll show you the manner of it. This shoe is my father: no, this left shoe is my father: no, no, this left shoe is my mother: nay, that cannot be so neither: yes, it is so, it is so, it hath the worser sole. This shoe, with the hole in it, is my mother, and this my father; a vengeance **on't**! there 'tis: now, sit, this **staff** is my sister, for, look you, she is as white as a lily and as small as a wand: this hat is Nan, our maid: I am the dog — no, the dog is himself, and I am the dog — Oh! The dog is me, and I am myself; ay, so, so. Now come I to my father; Father, your blessing: now should not the shoe speak a word for weeping: now should I kiss my father; well, he weeps on. Now come I to my mother: O, that she could speak now like a **wood** woman! Well, I kiss her; why, there 'tis; here's my mother's breath up and down. Now come I to my sister; mark the moan she makes. Now the dog all this while sheds not a tear nor speaks a word; but see how I lay the dust with my tears!

KING LEAR ACT I SCENE 2

Background:	*King Lear* is a play about family and the way children and parents treat one another.
	Edmund is the illegitimate son of Gloucester and the half-brother of Edgar. Knowing that he will never inherit, Edmund wants to cause Gloucester to hate Edgar so much that he gives everything to Edmund.
Character:	Edmund is willing to do whatever it takes to get what he wants. There is no love for either his father or his brother. He is greedy, hasty, and impatient. But there is a definite glee in him as well. He's looking forward to creating problems.
	Read **Act I scene one** to see how Gloucester refers to Edmund. Gloucester is somewhat insulting towards Edmund and basically acknowledges Edmund won't get anything.
	Edmund has been away for nine years and Gloucester is about to send him away again. How would you feel if it was *your* father talking about you this way?
Tips:	Do you know anyone who would do anything to get ahead? What types of characteristics do they have? How do they look, act, talk? Are they strong, tall and confident? Are they quiet, sly and sneaky? Put these characteristics into the physical side of your character.
	In this monologue Edmund talks about how he prefers nature's rules instead of civil rules. That way he can make things up as he goes along and not follow tradition.
	Strive to put a sense of glee into the piece. Though Edmund is evil, he can have a charming side as well. He enjoys being the 'bad guy.'
	Edmund is going to give Gloucester a fake letter (supposedly from Edgar) which speaks against Gloucester. Will you have that letter out the whole time? Is there a point to bring it out of your pocket slowly? Does he dance with the letter? Cradle it? Hold it high? Carry it carefully or carelessly? You decide!

VOCABULARY

wherefore	why	**doth**	does
plague of custom	tradition dictates that illegitimate children cannot inherit property	**fops**	fools
lag	behind	**'tween**	between
base	low, illegitimate	**speed**	succeed

EDMUND

Thou, nature, art my goddess; to thy law
My services are bound. **Wherefore** should I
Stand in the **plague of custom**, and permit
The curiosity of nations to deprive me,
For that I am some twelve or fourteen moon-shines
Lag of a brother? Why bastard? Wherefore **base**?
When my dimensions are as well compact,
My mind as generous, and my shape as true,
As honest madam's issue? Why brand they us
With base? With baseness? Bastardy? Base, base?
Who, in the lusty stealth of nature, take
More composition and fierce quality
Than **doth** within a dull, stale, tired bed,
Go to the creating a whole tribe of **fops**,
Got '**tween** asleep and wake? Well, then,
Legitimate Edgar, I must have your land:
Our father's love is to the bastard Edmund
As to the legitimate: fine word, — legitimate!
Well, my legitimate, if this letter **speed**,
And my invention thrive, Edmund the base
Shall top the legitimate. I grow; I prosper:
Now, gods, stand up for bastards!

LOVE'S LABOURS LOST ACT 4 SCENE 3

Background:	King Ferdinand invites three young men (Berowne, Dumain, and Longaville) to his court with some very specific conditions: they must only sleep three hours a night, they must fast once a week, and they must swear off women.
	By **Act IV** all the men, including the King, have fallen madly in love and have taken to lamenting their condition.
	In the moment before this monologue the King finds out about Dumain and Longaville and chastises them both for breaking the pact. During this, Berowne has been in hiding. After listening to the King, he comes forward and scolds all three.
	In this monologue it's clear Berowne pretends that he alone has been faithful. Immediately following this monologue it is revealed to the group that he too is in love.
Character:	Berowne is a young lord. In this monologue he almost gives a sermon on the evil of those who break oaths knowing full well that he has done it too. What does that say about his personality that he feels comfortable pretending he's better than the others?
	Note: His name is "Biron" in some editions of the play.
Tips:	Read the full scene **(Act IV scene three)** to see how each of the men come in full of love and lamentation.
	Right before Berowne's speech, the King lashes out at the other two for their lack of fortitude. Think about what Berowne does as he listens to the King.
	Does he work himself up into a frenzy? Does he know he's also done wrong and decides to make himself look good? Does he want to make himself look like a hero in the King's eyes?
	There is some difficulty in the form of the speech because of the rhyming couplets. Don't get caught in repeating the same rhythm for every line. Are there moments where you can breathe in the middle of a line instead of at the end?
	Berowne mentions four men in the speech: Hercules: Known for his physical strength. Solomon: King of Israel, known especially for being wise. Nestor: The oldest and wisest of the Greeks during the Trojan war. Timon (of Athens): A misanthrope. He hated mankind.

VOCABULARY

leige	king	**teen**	grief
perjured	lied to	**gnat**	tiny bug, insignificant
o'ershot	overshot (archery term)	**gig**	a two-wheeled carriage drawn by one horse
mote	a speck	**caudle**	a thin soup for the sick

BEROWNE

Now step I forth to whip hypocrisy.
(he steps forward)
Ah, good my **liege**, I pray thee, pardon me!
Good heart, what grace hast thou, thus to reprove
These worms for loving, that art most in love?
Your eyes do make no coaches; in your tears
There is no certain princess that appears;
You'll not be **perjured**, 'tis a hateful thing;
Tush, none but minstrels like of sonneting!
But are you not ashamed? Nay, are you not,
All three of you, to be thus much **o'ershot**?
You found his **mote**; the king your mote did see;
But I a beam do find in each of three.
O, what a scene of foolery have I seen,
Of sighs, of groans, of sorrow and of **teen**!
O me, with what strict patience have I sat,
To see a king transformed to a **gnat**!
To see great Hercules whipping a **gig**,
And profound Solomon to tune a jig,
And Nestor play at push-pin with the boys,
And critic Timon laugh at idle toys!
Where lies thy grief, O, tell me, good Dumain?
And gentle Longaville, where lies thy pain?
And where my liege's? All about the breast:
A **caudle**, ho!

JULIUS CAESAR ACT 3 SCENE 1

Background:	A group of men (called the conspirators) believe that Julius Caesar is a bad ruler who is letting ambition get the best of him. The conspirators kill Caesar on March 15th, the "ides of March." Some of the conspirators believe that Marc Antony, Caesar's right hand man, is a threat. However, Brutus calls Antony a "limb" **(Act II scene one)** of Caesar. Brutus believes, wrongly, that once Caesar dies, Antony will wilt. The monologue takes place right after Caesar's murder. In the moment before, Antony has pleaded for his life, telling the conspirators he thought Caesar was "dangerous." Antony then asks that he be allowed to transport Caesar's body to the marketplace. The conspirators leave Antony alone with Caesar's body.
Character:	Marc Antony is a fascinating character. He is a clear friend of Caesar's, but when Caesar is murdered, Antony sides with the killers to save his own life. Later on in the play, he incites the Roman crowd to revolt against the conspirators. Antony ends up ruling Rome along with two others (not the conspirators). He's the consummate improviser and is not beneath deceit. He has often been described as a politician. How does this information influence the way you might perform the speech?
Tips:	In the monologue, Antony talks to the dead body of Julius Caesar — "thou bleeding piece of earth." Where is the body? What does it look like? Is it covered? Does Antony kneel beside it? Does he keep his distance? How does Antony change from the moment before, when he is pleading for his life, to now, when he is alone with the body? Does he sink to the floor before speaking? Is he calm and cool? Read the moment before and see how Antony portrays himself publicly and then privately. In the previous speech Antony calls the conspirators "honourable men," here he calls them "butchers." You should also read the beginning of **Act III scene one** where the conspirators kill Caesar. In the monologue Antony calls on an oath that the world should be turned upside-down for what the conspirators have done and that Caesar's ghost should come after them. Will you do this dramatically? Quietly? With fury? It has a ritualistic feel to it — how can you bring this into your performance?

VOCABULARY

ope	open	**custom of fell deeds**	cruelness grown familiar
cumber	hinder, burden	**Ate**	Goddess of Discord
so in use	so common	**let slip**	unleash
quarter'd	cut into four	**carrion**	dead - image of rotting flesh

MARC ANTONY

O, pardon me, thou bleeding piece of earth,
That I am meek and gentle with these butchers!
Thou art the ruins of the noblest man
That ever lived in the tide of times.
Woe to the hand that shed this costly blood!
Over thy wounds now do I prophesy,
Which, like dumb mouths, do **ope** their ruby lips,
To beg the voice and utterance of my tongue—
A curse shall light upon the limbs of men;
Domestic fury and fierce civil strife
Shall **cumber** all the parts of Italy;
Blood and destruction shall be **so in use**
And dreadful objects so familiar
That mothers shall but smile when they behold
Their infants **quarter'd** with the hands of war;
All pity choked with **custom of fell deeds**:
And Caesar's spirit, ranging for revenge,
With **Ate** by his side come hot from hell,
Shall in these confines with a monarch's voice
Cry 'Havoc,' and **let slip** the dogs of war;
That this foul deed shall smell above the earth
With **carrion** men, groaning for burial.

CYMBELINE ACT 2 SCENE 2

Background:	A bet is made that Jachimo can seduce Posthumus' wife, Imogen. After the direct approach ends up with Imogen flat-out rejecting Jachimo, he resorts to trickery. Much like the "Trojan Horse" story, Jachimo hides in a trunk and has Imogen place it in her bedroom, thinking it belongs to Posthumus.

As she sleeps, Jachimo emerges from the trunk to write down details that will convince Posthumus he knows Imogen intimately. |
| **Character:** | Jachimo is described as a noble gentleman from Italy. He's pretty much used to getting his own way, which is why he feels there's nothing wrong with tricking both Imogen and Posthumus. Read the scene of the wager between Posthumus and Jachimo in **Act I scene four**.

He is a villain but a charming one. I would describe him as wicked as opposed to evil. There is a sense of fun and game play in him. In fact, he comes clean on what he's done later in the play.

This character is sometimes listed as "Iachimo." |
| **Tips:** | Read the scene where Imogen rebukes Jachimo for trying to seduce her in **Act I scene six**.

One thing to remember is that Jachimo is taken with Imogen. "All of her that is out of doors most rich!" He would like to have an affair with her, despite the bet. When he is writing down the details of her room, he wants to kiss her but doesn't. He knows she is something he can never have without deceit.

Remember the time of night. At the end of the monologue the clock strikes three, and there is a sleeping person in the room. This will affect the way you move and speak. Is there any point in the monologue where he can speak too loudly and almost wake Imogen?

Remember too that at the beginning of the monologue Jachimo comes out of a trunk.

Jachimo mentions a couple of names: <u>Tarquin</u> is a Roman who took advantage a woman named Lucrece, <u>Cytherea</u> is another name for Venus. <u>Tereus</u> is a king who took advantage of his sister-in-law, Philomela (do you notice a theme here?) and cut out her tongue. |

VOCABULARY

rushes	leaves used as floor coverings	**azure**	sky-blue
ere	before	**arras**	wall hangings
unparagon'd	having no equal. Jachimo is saying Imogen is more perfect than rubies	**ape**	mimic
o' the taper	of the candle	**raven's eye**	a sign of sunrise

JACHIMO

The crickets sing, and man's o'er-labour'd sense
Repairs itself by rest. Our Tarquin thus
Did softly press the **rushes, ere** he waken'd
The chastity he wounded. Cytherea,
How bravely thou becomest thy bed, fresh lily,
And whiter than the sheets! That I might touch!
But kiss; one kiss! Rubies **unparagon'd**,
How dearly they do't! 'Tis her breathing that
Perfumes the chamber thus: the flame **o' the taper**
Bows toward her, and would under-peep her lids,
To see the enclosed lights, now canopied
Under these windows, white and **azure** laced
With blue of heaven's own tint. But my design,
To note the chamber: I will write all down:
Such and such pictures; there the window; such
The adornment of her bed; the **arras**; figures,
Why, such and such; and the contents o' the story.
Ah, but some natural notes about her body,
Above ten thousand meaner moveables
Would testify, to enrich mine inventory.
O sleep, thou **ape** of death, lie dull upon her!
And be her sense but as a monument,
Thus in a chapel lying!
Why should I write this down, that's riveted,
Screw'd to my memory? She hath been reading late
The tale of Tereus; here the leaf's turn'd down
Where Philomel gave up. I have enough:
To the trunk again, and shut the spring of it.
Swift, swift, you dragons of the night, that dawning
May bare the **raven's eye!** I lodge in fear;
Though this a heavenly angel, hell is here.
(A clock strikes)
One, two, three: time, time!

HENRY IV PART 2 ACT 4 SCENE 5

Background:	A play in the War of the Roses cycle where two families (York and Lancaster) fight for control of England.
	Henry the Sixth is dying. He's afraid his son Henry (called "Hal" by his friends) will be a bad king because he's never taken any responsibility in his life.
	In this monologue, Prince Henry sits by his dying father's bedside. It is in this speech that Henry steps up and accepts his duty. He becomes a king.
Character:	Henry has been pretending to be a party boy for most of the two parts of *Henry IV*. The King doesn't see it as an act, but Henry clearly does as he clarifies in **Henry IV Part 1, Act I scene two**.
Tips:	While Henry is starting to grow up, is there a longing for the life that he has lead? He knows that once he becomes king he must leave his other life and his friends behind. Do you see him as only looking forward in this speech, or both looking forward and looking back?
	Read the conversation between Henry and his father which occurs later in the scene. It's easily relatable to modern times. The conversation is about a father's relationship with his son. The father sees only the boy and not the man. The son only wants his father's approval. Do you know someone who has this relationship with their father? How do they act?
	In the middle of the monologue, Henry notices that a feather does not move on his father's lips and thinks his father has died. In **Act II scene two** Henry talks about how it would be hypocritical to cry over his father's sickness. How does this compare with the emotions Henry undergoes in this moment?
	A possible prop for the piece is a crown. Henry notices the crown lying by his father's head and, when he believes his father has died, he places the crown on his own head. How will you play this moment? With resentment? With sorrow? Or with a readiness to take on the responsibility of king?

VOCABULARY

perturbation	confusion	**perforce**	unavoidably
ports	gates	**rigol**	circle - the crown
biggen	nightcap, hat	**filial**	due from a son
suspire	breathe	**lineal**	descendants, line of descent

PRINCE HENRY

Why doth the crown lie there upon his pillow,
Being so troublesome a bedfellow?
O polish'd **perturbation**! Golden care
That keep'st the **ports** of slumber open wide
To many a watchful night! Sleep with it now!
Yet not so sound and half so deeply sweet
As he whose brow with homely **biggen** bound
Snores out the watch of night. O majesty!
When thou dost pinch thy bearer, thou dost sit
Like a rich armour worn in heat of day,
That scalds with safety. By his gates of breath
There lies a downy feather which stirs not:
Did he **suspire**, that light and weightless down
Perforce must move. My gracious lord! My father!
This sleep is sound indeed, this is a sleep
That from this golden **rigol** hath divorced
So many English kings. Thy due from me
Is tears and heavy sorrows of the blood,
Which nature, love, and **filial** tenderness,
Shall, O dear father, pay thee plenteously:
My due from thee is this imperial crown,
Which, as immediate as thy place and blood,
Derives itself to me. Lo, here it sits,
Which God shall guard: and put the world's whole strength
Into one giant arm, it shall not force
This **lineal** honour from me: this from thee
Will I to mine leave, as 'tis left to me.

THE COMEDY OF ERRORS ACT 3 SCENE 2

Background:	This is a comedy about mistaken identity.
	The play takes place in Ancient Greece. Two sets of twin children (one set of gentlemen, both named *Antipholus*, and one set of servants, both named *Dromio*) are separated in a shipwreck. One set of master/servant ends up in Syracuse, the other set ends up in Ephesus.
	Years later, the "Syracuse" set go searching for their brothers and end up in Ephesus. Of course, they come across people who think they are the "Ephesus" set. Confusion and hilarity ensue.
	In this monologue Antipholus of Syracuse has just met Luciana. Luciana is Antipholus of Ephesus' sister-in-law and that's who she thinks she's talking to. She wants him to be nicer to his wife, Adriana. Antipholus from Syracuse has no idea who Adriana is, and has in fact, fallen in love with Luciana.
Character:	Antipholus of Syracuse is the twin who has decided to search out his long lost brother. It seems bizarre that he doesn't clue-in to the moments of mistaken identity, especially since he and his brother have the same name!
	But there has to be a suspension of disbelief with the story and the character. There is a sense of naiveté and superstition in Antipholus; later on in the play he will blame the odd occurrences on the supernatural, still not thinking about his lost twin.
Tips:	This is a love monologue and out-of-context is quite sweet. In context however, there is a lot of comic potential as Antipholus tries to convince Luciana he's not married to her sister and that he loves her.
	Despite the odd circumstances, there is definitely a sense of romance and sincerity on Antipholus' part. He is not trying to be unkind to Adriana (which Luciana will certainly think he's being) but in his world, he has just met and fell in love with Luciana.
	Think about what Luciana's reaction to this speech would be. Luciana would probably become more and more distressed with every word Antipholus speaks. How does he deal with her reaction? Would she try to leave in the middle of the speech? How would he prevent her from leaving?

VOCABULARY

hit of mine	know my name	**mermaid**	mermaids enticed sailors to the rocks where they would drown
conceit	vanity	**siren**	same as mermaid
homage	respect	**dote**	show fondness for
train	entice, lure	**supposition**	opinion

ANTIPHOLUS OF SYRACUSE

Sweet mistress — what your name is else, I know not,
Nor by what wonder you do **hit of mine**,
Less in your knowledge and your grace you show not
Than our earth's wonder, more than earth divine.
Teach me, dear creature, how to think and speak;
Lay open to my earthy-gross **conceit**,
Smother'd in errors, feeble, shallow, weak,
The folded meaning of your words' deceit.
Against my soul's pure truth why labour you
To make it wander in an unknown field?
Are you a god? Would you create me new?
Transform me then, and to your power I'll yield.
But if that I am I, then well I know
Your weeping sister is no wife of mine,
Nor to her bed no **homage** do I owe
Far more, far more to you do I decline.
O, **train** me not, sweet **mermaid**, with thy note,
To drown me in thy sister's flood of tears:
Sing, **siren**, for thyself and I will **dote**:
Spread o'er the silver waves thy golden hairs,
And as a bed I'll take them and there lie,
And in that glorious **supposition** think
He gains by death that hath such means to die:
Let Love, being light, be drowned if she sink!

KING LEAR ACT 4 SCENE 2

Background:	Before retiring, King Lear wants to divide up his land and marry off his three daughters: Goneril, Regan and Cordelia. He will give the biggest dowry to the daughter who proclaims her love the most. Cordelia says she loves her father no more or no less than she should. This is not the right answer. Lear gives her nothing and divides the land equally between his daughters Goneril and Regan who gave extremely loving responses. Over the course of the play it is clear that Goneril and Regan have no love for their father. Goneril will do anything to get ahead including planning the death of her pushover of a husband, the Duke of Albany. She calls him "milk-liver'd" in this scene, meaning "cowardly." By this point in the play, Albany has had enough and is finally willing to verbalize the evil in Goneril's character.
Character:	Albany becomes an increasingly sympathetic character as the play goes on. He is less greedy and certainly less cruel than the other players, but not without flaws. He deliberately turns his back on what Goneril does because of his supposed love for her. He is generally calm and cool. But this speech comes too late to do much good. He could have stepped in when Goneril forced Lear out of her house, but said nothing at the time. Read this moment in **Act I scene four**.
Tips:	This monologue represents an outburst of emotion from Albany. He must realise what a fool he has been. This outburst has been building and growing inside of him. He is finally standing up to Goneril and calling her evil ways out. He experiences a transformation, which we should see in this exact moment. In the moment before this speech Goneril kisses another man. The stage directions indicate that Albany enters after the kiss, but what if he sees it? How does that affect the speech? Albany talks about how Goneril is willing to cut herself off from Lear in order to get ahead — "She that herself will sliver and disbranch."

VOCABULARY

disposition	your nature i.e. Goneril's evil nature	**perforce**	unavoidably
contemns	despises	**vile**	disgusting
sliver and disbranch	cut off	**head-lugg'd**	dragged by the head
material sap	he is referring to Lear	**madded**	made insane

ALBANY

O Goneril!
You are not worth the dust which the rude wind
Blows in your face. I fear your **disposition**:
That nature, which **contemns** its origin,
Cannot be border'd certain in itself;
She that herself will **sliver and disbranch**
From her **material sap**, **perforce** must wither
And come to deadly use.
Wisdom and goodness to the **vile** seem vile:
Filths savour but themselves. What have you done?
Tigers, not daughters, what have you perform'd?
A father, and a gracious aged man,
Whose reverence even the **head-lugg'd** bear would lick,
Most barbarous, most degenerate, have you **madded**.
Could my good brother suffer you to do it?
A man, a prince, by him so benefited!
If that the heavens do not their visible spirits
Send quickly down to tame these vile offences,
It will come,
Humanity must perforce prey on itself,
Like monsters of the deep.

THE TEMPEST ACT 2 SCENE 2

Background:	Prospero causes a storm which shipwrecks the King of Naples's ship. Trinculo is on board and ends up alone on one part of the island. He comes across the monster Caliban who, on seeing Trinculo, thinks that he is a spirit and tries to hide. The monologue details Trinculo's interaction with Caliban, as Trinculo tires to figure out who and what Caliban is.
Character:	Trinculo is often defined as a "jester" in the character list. He is a clown. I get the impression that Trinculo is someone who tries to be smarter than he is, and thus comes off looking twice as dumb.
Tips:	First off, think of how you want to portray Trinculo physically. How does he move? Do some research on the different types of clowns. Clowns are quite physical and this could prove useful in coming up with actions within the speech. Which is Trinculo? Is he a Commedia dell'Arte character? A slapstick type? Is he more like Charlie Chaplin? How can you use this information to affect the physical nature of the character? How afraid of the weather is Trinculo? Remember that he has just been shipwrecked. This fear of the storm could lead to some interesting comic moments. If Trinculo is terrified of another storm, how would that affect the opening and his entrance? Trinculo makes an interesting comment about mankind when he says that men will not give money to a homeless person, and yet will pay handsomely to see some side-show character. But he also thinks that if he had Caliban in England, that Caliban would make him a lot of money.

VOCABULARY

I'the	in the	**doit**	small coin
yond	over there	**warm o' my troth**	by my word
bombard	leather bottle	**gabardine**	cloak
Poor-John	fried fish	**hereabouts**	near this place

TRINCULO

Here's neither bush nor shrub, to bear off any weather at all, and another storm brewing; I hear it sing **i' the** wind: **yond** same black cloud, yond huge one, looks like a foul **bombard** that would shed his liquor. If it should thunder as it did before, I know not where to hide my head: yond same cloud cannot choose but fall by pailfuls. *(seeing Caliban)* What have we here? A man or a fish? Dead or alive? *(he takes a big sniff)* A fish: he smells like a fish; a very ancient and fish-like smell; a kind of not of the newest **Poor-John**. A strange fish! Were I in England now, as once I was, and had but this fish painted, not a holiday fool there but would give a piece of silver: there would this monster make a man; any strange beast here makes a man: when they will not give a **doit** to relieve a lame beggar, they will lazy out ten to see a dead Indian. Legged like a man and his fins like arms! **Warm o' my troth!** I do now let loose my opinion; hold it no longer: this is no fish, but an islander, that hath lately suffered by a thunderbolt.
(looks up as if he hears thunder)
Alas, the storm is come again! My best way is to creep under his **gabardine**; there is no other shelter **hereabouts**: misery acquaints a man with strange bed-fellows!

TITUS ANDRONICUS ACT 2 SCENE 3

Background:	Titus Andronicus is a war hero. He returns from a victory over the Goths, bringing Tamora (Queen of the Goths) with him. As a sacrifice to the gods, Titus kills one of Tamara's sons. In revenge, Tamora and her boyfriend Aaron secretly set out to destroy Titus and his family.
	In this speech Aaron outlines the plan for the murder of Bassianus and for the ravaging of Titus' daughter (Lavinia) by Tamara's sons. Afterwards, Lavinia's hands will be cut off and her tongue will be removed so she cannot name her tormenters.
Character:	Aaron is a Goth. He is described as the "beloved" of Tamora and in this speech he calls her "the empress of my soul."
	Aaron has a one-track mind, though; Tamora wants to share a moment with him while they are alone but he is too focused on murder to think of love.
Tips:	The monologue takes place in an isolated part of the forest.
	This character is pure evil. Aaron tells Tamora that though she is thinking of love, he can think of nothing but coldness (the significance of Saturn), vengeance and death.
	How will you portray this strong characteristic? Think of how you can use opposite emotions to make the speech more chilling. It's easy to play a ranting fool, it cuts to the bone to see someone charming or pleasant say awful, disgusting things.
	I also see the tone of the piece as slow and deadly. Aaron is completely focused on killing and certainly doesn't rush into things. This should be conveyed in the way you speak.
	Having said that, it's interesting that someone so evil can love so deeply. What does this say about Aaron and his relationship with Tamora? Or do love and evil become equal in this case?
	To add another layer, later on in the play (**Act IV scene two**) Aaron goes to great lengths to try and save the life of his son.
	Aaron mentions the name <u>Philomel</u> — a mythological character who was raped and had her tongue cut out so she could not speak.

VOCABULARY

deadly-standing	death stare	**venereal**	lustful
adder	deadly snake	**pillage**	rob, a war term

AARON

Madam, though Venus govern your desires,
Saturn is dominator over mine:
What signifies my **deadly-standing** eye,
My silence and my cloudy melancholy,
My fleece of woolly hair that now uncurls
Even as an **adder** when she doth unroll
To do some fatal execution?
No, madam, these are no **venereal** signs:
Vengeance is in my heart, death in my hand,
Blood and revenge are hammering in my head.
Hark Tamora, the empress of my soul,
Which never hopes more heaven than rests in thee,
This is the day of doom for Bassianus:
His Philomel must lose her tongue to-day,
Thy sons make **pillage** of her chastity
And wash their hands in Bassianus' blood.

AS YOU LIKE IT ACT 2 SCENE 6

Background:	Orlando must flee his home because his brother, Oliver, means him harm. He has no money and no prospects, but Adam, Orlando's servant, offers to pay for their journey just to get Orlando out of harm's way.
	Orlando and Adam have just entered Arden forest. It has been a tough journey. In the moment before this speech Adam has stated he can go no further because he will "die for food." The monologue is Orlando's response.
Character:	We first meet Orlando at the top of the play complaining about how his brother Oliver has kept him locked up. We then see him in **Act I scene two** where he fights the enormous wrestler, Charles. It is in this scene that Orlando and Rosalind meet and fall instantly in love.
	Orlando was supposed to lose the fight and because he didn't, Oliver is even more furious. He wants to arrange Orlando's death. Adam finds out about this. He and Orlando decide to run away to the forest. (**Act II scene three**)
	While in the forest, Orlando spends most of his time writing bad love poetry for Rosalind and hanging it on trees. It is Rosalind herself, disguised as Ganymede, who teaches Orlando to be the perfect boyfriend.
	Orlando is the typical handsome leading man. He has been harshly treated by his older brother and yet does not seem bitter. He is also very loyal. Is Orlando the perfect gentleman, or a bit of a dunce? What is your opinion of him?
Tips:	Since Orlando spends most of the play mooning over Rosalind, this speech represents a nice change. Even though he is the consummate romantic, it's good to see he has a sense of humour!
	While Orlando is not making fun of Adam in this speech (remember the qualities of his character) he's certainly having some fun with him. Let that playfulness really come out.
	At the same time, keep in mind that Orlando truly cares for Adam.

VOCABULARY

comfort a little	take heart	**mocker**	one who ridicules
uncouth	strange, wild	**well said**	well done
conceit	vanity, imagination	**cheerly**	cheerfully
powers	abilities	**liest**	lie

ORLANDO

Why, how now, Adam! No greater heart in thee? Live a little; **comfort a little**; cheer thyself a little. If this **uncouth** forest yield any thing savage, I will either be food for it or bring it for food to thee. Thy **conceit** is nearer death than thy **powers**. For my sake be comfortable; hold death awhile at the arm's end: I will here be with thee presently; and if I bring thee not something to eat, I will give thee leave to die: but if thou diest before I come, thou art a **mocker** of my labour. **Well said**, thou lookest **cheerly**, and I'll be with thee quickly. Yet thou **liest** in the bleak air: come, I will bear thee to some shelter; and thou shalt not die for lack of a dinner, if there live anything in this desert. Cheerly, good Adam!

CYMBELINE ACT 5 SCENE 4

Background:	Posthumus had been banished for marrying Cymbeline's daughter, Imogen. He has been caught in Britain and sentenced to death. The Jailor arrives to take Posthumus to the gallows.
Character:	Here is a character about which nothing is known! He doesn't even have a name. He only appears in this one scene and his job is to take Posthumus to his death. Shakespeare has great skill at inserting comedic characters into his tragedies. The sky is the limit. You create the character from scratch. He can be whatever you imagine him to be.
Tips:	Even though it's a tragic moment for Posthumus, this is a comic monologue. It's very ironic that the Jailor talks about how much better off Posthumus will be when he dies. It's also clear that the Jailor is of the lower classes. Even though he's taking Posthumus to his death, he always addresses Posthumus as "sir." How will this class structure affect the way you move and talk? Think about the physical nature of this character. Again, the sky is the limit! Just don't be ordinary; remember you are trying to create a unique impression and the physical side of the character is just as important as the words. What an opening line! Is the Jailor making a joke? Is he serious? This line makes quite an entrance for the monologue and the character. How will you make your entrance? What tone will you set for your audience?

VOCABULARY

reckoning	to deal with	**debitor and creditor**	book of accounts
procuring	getting	**counters**	objects used in calculations
mirth	happy times	**acquittance**	payment of debt
penny cord	a hangman's rope	**gallowes**	execution by hanging

JAILOR

Come sir, are you ready for death? Hanging is the word, sir. If you be ready for that, you are well cooked. A heavy **reckoning** for you, sir. But the comfort is, you shall be called to no more payments, fear no more tavern-bills; which are often the sadness of parting, as the **procuring** of **mirth**: you come in faint for want of meat, depart reeling with too much drink; sorry that you have paid too much, and sorry that you are paid too much; purse and brain both empty; the brain the heavier for being too light, the purse too light, being drawn of heaviness: of this contradiction you shall now be quit. O, the charity of a **penny cord**! It sums up thousands in a trice: you have no true **debitor and creditor** but it; of what's past, is, and to come, the discharge: your neck, sir, is pen, book and **counters**; so the **acquittance** follows. Indeed, sir, he that sleeps feels not the tooth-ache: but a man that were to sleep your sleep, and a hangman to help him to bed, I think he would change places with his officer; for, look you, sir, you know not which way you shall go. What an infinite mock is this, that a man should have the best use of his eyes to see the way of blindness! I am sure hanging's the way of winking. O, there were desolation of jailers and **gallowses**!

NOTES

NOTES

Theatrefolk

Original Playscripts

PO Box 1064, Crystal Beach, ON, Canada L0S 1B0
Tel 1-866-245-9138 / Fax 1-877-245-9138
Email tfolk@theatrefolk.com / Web www.theatrefolk.com

To learn more about Theatrefolk, visit us on the World Wide Web

> Online Ordering
> Up-to-date Catalogue
> Royalty Information
> Company Background

WWW.**THEATREFOLK**.COM

Email: tfolk@theatrefolk.com